The Tattingstone Wonder, near Ipswich in Suffolk, was built to house estate workers, with a three-sided tower to act as an eyecatcher in the form of a mock church tower.

Follies

Jeffery W. Whitelaw

A Shire book

Published in 2005 by Shire Publications Ltd,
Cromwell House, Church Street, Princes Risborough,
Buckinghamshire HP27 9AA, UK.
(Website: www.shirebooks.co.uk)

Copyright © 1982, 1997 and 2005 by Jeffery W. Whitelaw.
First published 1982. Second edition 1990. Third edition
1997. Fourth edition, revised and updated with colour
illustrations, 2005.
Shire Album 93. ISBN 0 7478 0624 1.
Jeffery W. Whitelaw is hereby identified as the author of
this work in accordance with Section 77 of the Copyright,
Designs and Patents Act 1988.

British Library Cataloguing in Publication Data:
Whitelaw, Jeffery W.
Follies. – 4th ed. – (Shire album; 93)
1. Follies (Architecture) – Great Britain – History
I. Title 717
ISBN 0 7478 0624 1.

Cover: *In 1765 the fourth Earl of Dunmore built a pavilion overlooking the south-facing garden of his estate at Dunmore, Falkirk, but it was not until 1777, when he and his family were evacuated from the rebellious American colonies, where he had been the last British Governor of Virginia, that he returned to crown his summerhouse with an enormous stone pineapple, perhaps as a reminder of his reluctant tour of duty, or perhaps to emulate the custom of American sailors of returning home with the fruit. Cunningly designed to spill rainwater from stone leaf to stone leaf, it remains probably the most elaborate of all follies and is let as a holiday home by the Landmark Trust.*

ACKNOWLEDGEMENTS
Most of the photographs are by the author. The exceptions are acknowledged as follows:
Brian Dix, front cover; Cadbury Lamb, pages 1, 3 (left), 4, 9, 11, 12, 14, 19 (top and
centre), 20 (top), 22 (both), 23, 27 (bottom), 28, 29 (top), 31 (all), 33 (bottom), 34 (both), 35
(both), 38, 39, 42, 45 (bottom), 47 (top), 51 (bottom), 51 (all), 52, 54 (both), 59, 60 (bottom),
61 (both), 62; Suzanne Ross, page 57 (both), 63; G. N. Wright, page 26 (top).

Printed in Malta by Gutenberg Press Limited, Gudja Road,
Tarxien PLA 19, Malta.

Contents

Above left: *The Folly Bridge at Hartwell near Aylesbury in Buckinghamshire has been restored by Historic House Hotels working to plans by local architect Eric Throssell, whose research has enabled it to be reconstructed as originally built in the 1760s.*

Above right: *The Temple of Apollo, Stourhead, Wiltshire. The Stourhead estate was bought by the Hoare banking family in 1714, and Henry Hoare II, the son of the founder, created the magnificent gardens, today owned by the National Trust. To provide some fashionable buildings for the gardens, he employed the architect Henry Flitcroft, who designed the follies now known as the Temple of Flora (1744), the Pantheon (1754) and the Temple of Apollo (1765), as well as Alfred's Tower (1772 – see page 53).*

Foreword

It was in 1982 that I had the pleasure of seeing the first edition of this book published, with the illustrations in monochrome. Even though my stock of 'folly' illustrations today is in no way complete, at that time it was very small. When I started on the project I held no images of follies in several areas mentioned in the Gazetteer: I was indebted to friends, therefore, for illustrations where I could not supply them myself.

In 1990 and 1997 second and third printings were published, some of the illustrations being replaced and minor changes and additions being made to the Gazetteer each time. For this new and enlarged edition, I have kept to the original structure of the book – making revisions where necessary – but the main change, of course, is that the majority of the illustrations are now coloured, although a few monochromes have been retained. Secondly, a number of follies in Scotland and Wales – together with some in the Isles of Man and Wight – have been added, extending its geographical coverage.

Finally a few acknowledgements and apologies. I have made considerable use of the information contained in articles in the Folly Fellowship's magazines and journals, and I am also very grateful to the authors of other books on the subject which I have consulted for accuracy. I offer my humble apologies to any of them who may consider that I have used their words without acknowledgement.

Jeffery W. Whitelaw, 2005

Freston Tower, Freston, Suffolk, visible from the road to Shotley, stands on a hillside on the south bank of the river Orwell and may well be the oldest folly of all. Barbara Jones wrote that 'it may be the first prospect tower, built by Edward Latymer c.1579, or just possibly part of a demolished house', preserved for the view it gave of the shipping on the river. Six storeys high, with a single small room on each floor, the red brick tower has windows on the river side increasing in size closer to the top. There is a fanciful story that the tower was built as a place where Ellen de Freston was made to study, one floor being devoted to each subject! The tower was restored in 2003 by the Landmark Trust as a holiday home.

Follies in Britain

The late Barbara Jones, in her definitive book *Follies and Grottoes*, begins her introduction with these words: 'A folly might be defined as a useless building erected for ornament on a gentleman's estate'. She then went on to differentiate between a 'folly' and 'garden architecture' – although she did feel that the line between them was uncertain. No such distinction will be made here, however, because some of our finest follies are to be found in the great landscaped gardens of Britain – like those at Castle Howard, Stowe or Stourhead, where the gardens would not be the same without them.

Whether or not a building is a folly – be it belvedere, grotto, obelisk, pagoda, pavilion, prospect tower, pyramid, deliberately built ruin, sham castle or triumphal arch – depends on when and where it was built and why, and even whether it feels like a folly. Follies are linked by a departure from the general norm and the intention that they be looked at and enjoyed: they are buildings and structures made for pleasure and, in some cases, designed to give a livelier consequence to the landscape. Sir Hugh Casson wrote that 'the mark of a true folly is that it was erected to satisfy and give pleasure to the builder, and greatly to surprise the stranger'.

With follies taking many forms and built in unusual places, the reasons for some of them may be obscure. Although the rich men who built them did not need to give reasons, there are few follies without at least one story to justify their existence, sometimes arrived at by the local community at a later date for its own satisfaction.

Sometimes follies are inaccessible for their own protection; others have been difficult to reach because of the terrain but access to previously unattainable sites has been achieved through the efforts of The Folly Fellowship, a charity founded in 1988 to bring together all those with an interest in follies, grottoes and garden buildings.

The earliest building categorised as a 'folly' is Freston Tower, which was built *c.*1579 overlooking the river Orwell near Ipswich in Suffolk. It is considered to be the oldest prospect tower and, therefore, the oldest folly, although there is still a lingering doubt that this isolated tower might just be the remaining part of a long-demolished house.

If Freston Tower is not the first folly, that distinction must go to the remarkable building on the edge of the grounds of Rushton Hall in Northamptonshire known as the Triangular Lodge, and now in the care of English Heritage. It was begun in 1593 and finished in 1596, the brainchild of Sir Thomas Tresham (who was the father of Francis Tresham, one of the

The Triangular Lodge, Rushton, Northamptonshire, now in the care of English Heritage, is considered to be the earliest true folly. It was built in 1593–6 in the grounds of Rushton Hall, a few miles from Kettering, by Sir Thomas Tresham. Sir Thomas was a Catholic and had been imprisoned for his faith. While in prison he became obsessed with the Holy Trinity and this obsession drove him, when freed, to erect the Triangular Lodge, every detail of which is touched by the symbolism of three.

conspirators who planned the Gunpowder Plot of 1605), but he would not have considered that he was building anything in the nature of a folly: indeed, he would not have known the word in its present context. He was a very religious man, brought up as a Protestant but converted to Catholicism in 1580, and, after becoming obsessed with thoughts of the Holy Trinity during a spell in prison because of his faith, he built the Triangular Lodge, which underlines the concept of three.

In 1594, Sir Thomas also began a much larger building in what then would have been a remote spot near Oundle, now called Lyveden New Bield, again with number symbolism and built in the shape of a cross, but after his death in 1605 it was never finished. These two buildings in Northamptonshire, together with the Freston Tower and, in 1606, the Pepperbox, erected by Giles Eyre in Whiteparish in Wiltshire, are just early isolated

Lyveden New Bield, near Oundle, Northamptonshire, was another of Sir Thomas Tresham's creations, planned in the shape of a cross and built between 1594 and 1605 to represent his Catholic faith during the reign of Protestant Queen Elizabeth I. It is the only one of Tresham's buildings for which he employed an architect and the plans still survive. Elaborate friezework around the outside of the two-storey building tells the story of the Passion and the plans show that there was to be a vaulted roof finished by a large stone ball. Sir Thomas died in 1605 and, as his son Francis was involved in the Gunpowder Plot, the building was never finished. The roofless building is in the care of the National Trust and remains virtually unaltered after four hundred years.

Eyre's Folly, Whiteparish, Wiltshire. This hexagonal brick tower, one of the earliest follies, was erected by Giles Eyre in 1606 and, because of its shape, has become known as The Pepperbox, giving its name to the hill on which it stands. With the original ground-level arches and all the windows bricked in, there is no entry to the building but now it is – together with the hill – a National Trust property. From it there is a fine view overlooking Salisbury.

examples and there are no other follies recorded for more or less another century.

It was not until the late seventeenth and eighteenth centuries, when aristocrats or their sons returned from what was called the 'Grand Tour of Europe', that the building of follies began in earnest. Having seen ruins in what they considered to be romantic settings on the Continent, and in Italy in particular, they returned home determined to embellish the landscapes of their estates with reminders of classical Greece and Rome. Thus the desire to improve their estates by the addition of artificially created ruins became the fashion of the day. Landscape gardeners and architects such as Charles Bridgeman, Lancelot 'Capability' Brown, William Kent, Sir John Vanbrugh, James Gibbs and Nicholas Hawksmoor aided the landowners in their schemes.

These landowners were not only excited by their plans for the romanticising of their estates but found the building of sham ruins and other Gothic buildings answered a yearning for the violence and chivalry of the past. This 'pleasurable enjoyment of the grisly', as it has been called, was encouraged by the work of the Gothic poets and, later, by writers such as Horace Walpole, who, in a period of over twenty years in the second half of the century, built – starting with the house itself – a remarkable collection of Gothic follies on his Strawberry Hill House estate in Twickenham. The house, now a Roman Catholic college, remains but, except for the restored Chapel in the Woods, all his follies have disappeared.

At the beginning of the eighteenth century, Sir John Vanbrugh, who had already made a reputation as a soldier and a playwright, but who had had no formal training as an architect, designed Castle Howard in North Yorkshire and, with Nicholas Hawksmoor, embellished the grounds and the parkland with a variety of architectural structures, including a pyramid, a mausoleum and the Temple of the Four Winds. Finally, in 1709, he rounded off his whole grand design by building the first sham fortification, a great wall complete with eleven towers, which has remained the biggest folly in England.

In 1721 the first Earl Bathurst built Alfred's Hall in his grounds at Cirencester House and this, although little more than a much embellished cottage, is considered to be the first sham castle. The first deliberately ruinous sham castle was built by Sanderson Miller on his own estate at Radway Grange in Warwickshire. As a consequence, Miller acquired a reputation and was soon afterwards commissioned to build a ruin at Hagley in Worcestershire.

A cheaper alternative to building a sham castle was to erect the façade of a castle against a suitable farmhouse, especially if it was visible from the landowner's mansion. A good example is Stowe Castle in Buckinghamshire, a fine castle façade against a

Stowe Castle, Stowe, Buckinghamshire. The gardens at Stowe, in which can be seen work by Charles Bridgeman, James Gibbs, William Kent and 'Capability' Brown, were acquired by the National Trust in July 1989. They contain over thirty Grade 1 listed temples, monuments and follies. More than a mile from the house is an eyecatcher known as Stowe Castle – really a fortified and castellated wall covering a group of two-storeyed cottages – put up by Lord Cobham towards the end of his life.

Broadway Tower, Broadway, Worcestershire. Visible for many miles on eastward routes through the Vale of Evesham, the tower was designed by James Wyatt and completed in 1797 for the sixth Earl of Coventry. He decided to add to the follies on his estate at Croome by putting up a tower to 'animate the horizon'. It was later used by William Morris and Edward Burne-Jones for holidays and now contains an exhibition about its history.

farmhouse, built before 1738, and a foretaste of the politically motivated buildings and monuments of the gardens at Stowe. Another castle façade was built on Strattenborough Farm in 1792 as an eyecatcher for Coleshill Park in Oxfordshire. The farm remains but the hall was destroyed by fire in 1955. There are two elaborate examples in Cumbria, collectively known as Greystoke Castle. In 1780, the Duke of Norfolk, to honour the Americans after the War of Independence, embellished two farmhouses and cowhouses with elaborate castellations and called them 'Fort Putnam' and 'Bunkers Hill'.

Other screen façades were built to look like temples or churches, the most famous being the Tattingstone Wonder in Suffolk, a rare example of a folly designed not only as an eyecatcher but also with a functional and useful purpose. In 1760 Squire White, having built three cottages for some of his labourers, decided to follow the fashion of the day and make an eyecatcher, so he enclosed the side of the cottages that faced the Hall with what appears to be a flint and masonry church complete with a tower! Another good example of an eyecatcher is that for Rousham House in Oxfordshire. In 1738 William Kent began to create the great garden in Italianate style, complete with temples, statues, a pyramid house and rustic seats. He finished off his scheme with a castellated wall visible from the garden on the horizon.

A fine example of an eyecatcher is the huge belvedere that stands on Fish Hill, some 3 miles from the picturesque village of Broadway in the Cotswolds. In 1797 the Earl of Coventry, who had already adorned his estate at Croome Park with a variety of follies, decided to enliven the landscape and improve the view by building Broadway Tower. Fish Hill is some 15 miles from Croome and so, to test that the proposed eyecatcher would be seen from the Hall, his wife had a beacon lit on the intended site.

However, there were a few fortunate landowners who, when they came to landscape their estates in the fashion of the time, found that they had a genuine ruin already *in situ*. One of the earliest is the Rievaulx Terrace, near Helmsley in North Yorkshire, with a temple *c.*1758 at each end but with a ready-made eyecatcher in the form of the very imposing twelfth-century ruin of Rievaulx Abbey in the valley below. On a similar and somewhat larger scale, also in North Yorkshire, is Studley Royal garden with its follies and cascade, and a view of the spectacular twelfth-century Fountains Abbey.

Away from the large estates, a number of individual structures were being built at the time. These are what many would call true follies, and examples are the Bellmount Tower near Grantham in Lincolnshire (1749), the visible-for-miles sham ruin Mow Cop on the Cheshire–Staffordshire border (1750), Perrott's Folly at Edgbaston in Warwickshire (1758), The Pineapple at Dunmore in Scotland (1777), Old John Folly in Bradgate Park, Leicestershire (1786), and Horton Tower (1722) and Denis Bond's Grange Arch at Creech (1746) – both in Dorset.

The folly builders then, as later, were men of substance who could afford to indulge a monumental fancy. Some led fashion,

Mow Cop, near Congleton, Cheshire. This dramatically placed sham ruin was built in 1750 by Randle Wilbraham, who lived in the valley below. It stands on the Cheshire–Staffordshire border, some 1100 feet (335 metres) above sea level, 5 miles south of Congleton. It can be seen for many miles and from all directions.

others followed it, but never slavishly – even the ideas of great designers and architects were modified by the visions of their patrons – and many early follies were designed and executed by amateurs. When the Gothic passion began to dissipate, although the succeeding fashion for delicacy and grace was translated into tall elegant towers and grand triumphal arches, it was the amateurs, to whose follies such interesting tales belong and who built to please themselves or outdo their neighbours, who exploited the possibilities and provided the richest variety of style and form. And so it is in the later follies that their intrinsic singularity is most marked. Such follies are very personal. They can betray a mood, an attitude to life and society and a man's view of his status – and sometimes his income – as some curious buildings testify! Splendid eccentricities were put up, such as 'Jack the Treacle Eater' among the Barwick Park follies at Yeovil in Somerset, the lodge at Rendlesham in Suffolk, the miniature Stonehenge at Ilton, near Masham in North Yorkshire, and the follies of Mad Jack Fuller at Brightling and Dallington in Sussex.

In the industrial age some eccentric buildings such as Peterson's Tower at Sway in Hampshire and the Wainhouse Tower at Halifax were erected, and there were new opportunities for folly builders. One of the earliest, in 1840, was the mock castle façade, complete with turrets and castellations, over the entrance to Clayton Tunnel on the London to Brighton railway line. A different façade was created at Paddington in London when the Metropolitan Railway was extended in 1868: numbers 23 and 24 Leinster Gardens were demolished but their house fronts were retained to preserve the appearance of the road.

Druid's Temple, Ilton, near Masham, North Yorkshire. At the beginning of the nineteenth century, when the cult of the Druids was much in fashion, William Danby of Swinton Hall built a miniature Stonehenge on the edge of the moors above his home. There are other sham Druid's temples or stone circles elsewhere but this is the best and many have been deluded into believing it to be genuine.

The Hopetoun Monument, Haddington, East Lothian, stands at the junction of the A6137 north from the town with the Athelstaneford road. It celebrates the life of General John Hope, Earl of Hopetoun, and was built in 1824 with local funding from his tenants.

The twentieth century was certainly not conducive to folly building in the grand style although, following the major upheaval of the Second World War, when gardens were neglected or allowed to fall into decay, much restoration has taken place of several landscaped gardens, particularly since 1981 by the Painshill Park Trust at Painshill Park (off the A3 London to Guildford road) in Surrey; at the Rococo Garden at Painswick in Gloucestershire after an exhibition of eighteenth-century paintings in 1976 revived interest in the garden; by the National Trust at Prior Park at Bath; and at Stowe, where the Trust has undertaken the major task of repairing some of the thirty-two temples and monuments.

There is one great structure that was built in the true tradition of two centuries earlier – the 140 foot (43 metre) tower which Lord Berners created in 1935 at Faringdon in Oxfordshire. Times were very different and landowners were not locally all-powerful as they were in the past but, despite many objections and even a court of enquiry, Lord Berners did eventually achieve his goal: today he would never have obtained planning permission!

A gazetteer of follies

England

BEDFORDSHIRE

ASPLEY GUISE. Henry VII Lodge is what appears to be a Tudor building but the Duke of Bedford, in 1811, commissioned Humphry Repton and his son to re-create a fifteenth-century house from existing materials.

OLD WARDEN. The Swiss Garden was first laid out early in the nineteenth century by Lord Ongley and, although in 1872 the estate was bought by Joseph Shuttleworth, who continued to improve it, the Swiss Garden is now administered by the county council.

SOUTHILL. In 1777 'Capability' Brown was commissioned to landscape the estate, and here are a fishing temple, an obelisk, statues and a one-arch bridge.

WOBURN. The Chinese Dairy, the Shell Room Grotto, a pagoda and the Thornery Pavilion may be seen at Woburn Abbey, the ancestral home of the Dukes of Bedford.

WREST PARK, Silsoe. Formal gardens were laid out by the Duke of Kent in the early eighteenth century and here can be seen Archer's Pavilion (see below), the Orangery, the Bath House, Bowling Green House and the Chinese Bridge.

Archer's Pavilion at Wrest Park, Silsoe, Bedfordshire. The formal gardens at Wrest Park were laid out for the twelfth Earl Grey by Charles Bridgeman between 1706 and 1740 and Thomas Archer designed the pavilion between 1709 and 1711. Today it remains a grand eyecatcher to the house at the southern end of the Long Water, attended by a statue of William III.

Temple Island, Remenham, Berkshire. The temple on Temple Island in the River Thames consists of a building supporting a white rotunda which was built by James Wyatt in 1771. It acts as an eyecatcher to Fawley Court across the river in Buckinghamshire.

BERKSHIRE

BASILDON. The Peacock Pavilion and Fountain were set up near the River Thames at the Child-Beale Nature Reserve by Gilbert Child-Beale, who founded the reserve as a memorial to his parents.

REMENHAM. Temple Island (see above).

WINDSOR. In 1793 James Wyatt designed a Gothic temple in the grounds of Frogmore House for Queen Charlotte, George III's wife.

BUCKINGHAMSHIRE

BEACONSFIELD. Hall Barn was landscaped in the eighteenth century by John Aislabie (later the creator of Studley Royal). Here there is a temple of Venus, a fishing temple, a ruinous grotto, statues and an obelisk to commemorate the completion of the work *c.*1740. It is private property but visits may be arranged on application to the Estate Manager.

BOURNE END. Lord Boston's Folly, Hedsor, is a late-eighteenth-century flint sham castle comprising three towers – circular, hexagonal and square – situated on a hill to the east of Bourne End. It was built by Lord Boston in 1793 and tradition has it that he built it to celebrate George III's recovery from his first illness and also that it was designed by the king himself. It has now been converted into a home.

BUCKINGHAM. Lord Cobham's Castle. In order to qualify the town to hold its own assize, Lord Cobham built, in 1748, the Old Gaol, complete with turrets, trefoil windows and crenellations – a magnificent sham.

CHALFONT ST PETER. An obelisk was erected by Sir H. T. Gott in 1785 to commemorate the spot where George III killed a stag. It was also a beacon and records the distance to London and other towns.

CLIVEDEN. The house, once the home of Lady Astor, is administered by the National Trust and let out as a hotel. In the gardens are the Blenheim Pavilion, a gazebo and, on an island in the water gardens, an iron pagoda.

DINTON. Dinton Castle (see below).

FAWLEY. Fawley Court, originally built in 1684 and renovated in 1771, has gardens which were redesigned by 'Capability' Brown at the time of the renovation. Here can be seen the Dairy, a rusticated bridge and a large domed sham ruin.

HARTWELL. The grounds at Hartwell House, now owned by Historic House Hotels, have been painstakingly restored by them and contain a Gothic tower, an Ionic temple, the exterior of a Gothic church, a Folly Bridge (page 3), a column with a statue of George II on top, and an obelisk, all of the eighteenth century. In Lower Hartwell there is what is known as the Egyptian Spring, a wellhead designed by Joseph Bonomi in 1851.

Dinton Castle, Dinton, Buckinghamshire, stands beside the Aylesbury to Thame road, and, although much overgrown with nettles and overtopped by trees, it still fulfils part of its original purpose. It was built in 1769 by Sir John Vanhatten as an eyecatcher and to house his collection of ammonites and other fossils incorporated in the structure. The stairs and tower tops have long gone but some of the fossils can still be seen as part of the rubble walling.

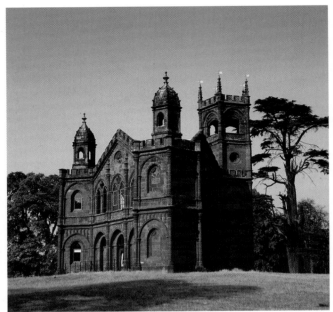

The Gothic Temple, Stowe, Buckinghamshire. Perhaps the best building in the gardens at Stowe, the Gothic Temple was designed by James Gibbs in 1741 but it was still not finished in 1748 and in 1756 Sanderson Miller records that Gibbs was at Stowe 'contriving a finishing to the building'. The temple was dedicated 'to the Liberties of our Ancestors' and, as the guide points out, the very Northamptonshire ironstone with which it is built – in contrast to most of the other classical temples – indicates 'Ancient Britain'. It has now been restored and rooms have been constructed inside so that the Landmark Trust can let it as a holiday home.

The Temple of British Worthies, Stowe, Buckinghamshire. When the area of the gardens where this temple is situated was being developed by William Kent in the 1730s, Lord Cobham wanted to give it a moral-political significance and an architectural frame to display the sixteen Immortal Britons in the form of busts and inscriptions. The stone busts, which include King Alfred, Queen Elizabeth I, Shakespeare, Sir Francis Drake and Milton, fall into two groups: on the left, those distinguished in the realm of ideas, and on the right, those revered for their actions.

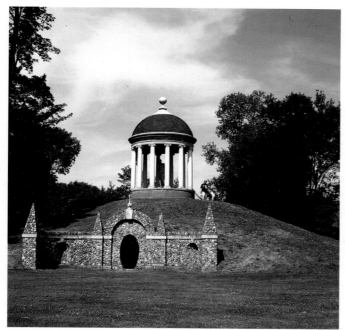

The Temple of Venus, West Wycombe Park, Buckinghamshire. Sir Francis Dashwood, afterwards Lord Le Despencer, inherited West Wycombe Park and in 1731 set about completely remodelling the house and grounds. After adding a golden ball to the tower of the church and creating the so-called Hell-Fire Caves, he turned his attention to the park, where he added a number of temples – the Temple of the Four Winds, the Temple of Bacchus, Daphne's Temple, the Temple of Music and, above all, the Temple of Venus. This is an Ionic rotunda, with a dome and ball finial, set on a mound above a flint tunnel archway. It was restored in 1984.

STOWE. In the Stowe Landscape Gardens and surrounding area there are over thirty listed temples, monuments and follies, including Stowe Castle (page 8), the Gothic Temple (page 16), the Temple of British Worthies (page 16), the Temple of Ancient Virtue, the Temple of Concord and Victory, the Temple of Venus, the Rotundo, the Doric Arch, the Palladian Bridge, the Cobham Monument, the Congreve Monument, the Grenville Column and the Chinese House.

WEST WYCOMBE. West Wycombe Park contains a number of follies including the Temple of Venus (see above), Daphne's Temple, the Temple of the Winds, the Arch of Apollo, the Dovecote Temple and the Temple of Music. St Lawrence's church, on the hilltop north of the road, has a golden ball on the tower; nearby is the Dashwood Mausoleum and at the bottom of the hill are the Hell-Fire Caves. On one of the estate cottages, called St Crispin's, there is a sham church tower.

WOTTON UNDERWOOD. Wotton House has several structures, mostly around its lake, including a Turkish tent, a classical rotunda and the Octagon Temple, which have all been restored. Other garden buildings include a five-arch bridge built by Sanderson Miller in 1758.

CAMBRIDGESHIRE

ABBOTS RIPTON. In the grounds of Ripton Hall, Peter Foster has been designing modern follies for Lord de Ramsey since 1954.

BURGHLEY HOUSE. Here, at the celebrated venue of the horse trials held every September, 'Capability' Brown created not only a perfect landscape but also designed the Gothick Orangery and the neo-Jacobean Bath House (really a summerhouse) in 1756, together with the Lion Bridge, a dairy and an icehouse.

The Kennels, Milton Park, Peterborough, Cambridgeshire. A most imposing feature is the sham medieval gatehouse façade to the kennels on the east side of the park, and it is thought that William Chambers was responsible for this as well as the temple in the park. The temple was completed in 1775 but, after collapsing in a storm in the latter half of the nineteenth century, was rebuilt as recently as 1986. The park, just outside Peterborough, is private property and not normally open to the public.

GRANTCHESTER. There is a sham castle in the garden of The Old Vicarage, which was once the home of Rupert Brooke.

MILTON PARK. In the private grounds of the Fitzwilliam estate between Castor and Peterborough, there are a Gothic lodge, a temple designed by Sir William Chambers in 1775 (rebuilt in 1986) and The Kennels (above).

WIMPOLE PARK. Sham Castle (see below).

Sham Castle, Wimpole Park, Cambridgeshire. The first Earl of Hardwicke bought the Wimpole estate, 8 miles southeast of Cambridge, in 1740, when he was Lord Chancellor. Impressed by the sham castle at Hagley, he commissioned Sanderson Miller to build one for him at Wimpole. After much delay, it was built between 1768 and 1772, but only after the second Lord Hardwicke had succeeded to the title. Wimpole Hall now belongs to the National Trust and the castle can be seen from the minor road to Great Eversden, east of the estate, or from the hall itself.

White Nancy, Bollington, Cheshire. This outstanding white-painted landmark is a cone-shaped stone building, about 12 feet (3.6 metres) high, on Kerridge Hill on the edge of High Peak. White Nancy was built in 1817 by a Colonel Gaskell as a boundary mark and to commemorate the Duke of Wellington's victory at Waterloo.

CHESHIRE

BOLLINGTON. White Nancy (see above).
LYME PARK, Disley. The Cage (see right)
MOW COP. Mow Cop (see page 10).

CORNWALL

MORWENSTOW. Hawker's Rectory: in the mid nineteenth century the Reverend Robert Stephen Hawker built this rectory with chimneys in the shape of his favourite church towers.
MOUNT EDGCUMBE. An eighteenth-century sham ruin overlooks Plymouth Sound (see below). Here also are an orangery, Milton's Temple and a shell seat (restored in 1990).

Above: *The Cage, Lyme Park, Disley, Cheshire. The history of the Lyme Park estate, now owned by the National Trust, goes back six hundred years and the Cage was originally built in 1580 as a very large hunting box, from which the ladies of the house watched the progress of the hunt. At some stage it became a lock-up – hence its name. It was restored in 1726 by Giacomo Leoni, who also added the towers.*

Left: *The Sham Ruin, Mount Edgcumbe, Cornwall. The park and gardens at Mount Edgcumbe, the earliest landscaped park in Cornwall, are owned jointly by Cornwall County Council and Plymouth City Council. The public are free to walk throughout the park and see, among other structures, this sham ruin of c. 1750.*

Left: *The Egyptian House, Chapel Street, Penzance, Cornwall, was built in 1830 by John Foulston for George Lavin to house a collection of minerals and reflects the contemporary vogue for Egyptian design.*

Below: *The Knill Monument, St Ives, Cornwall. This pyramid-like monument was built by John Knill in 1811 on Worvas Hill overlooking St Ives harbour, and the three sides have inscriptions cut into them, together with coats of arms. Knill was determined that his name should live on and at his death he left property to provide funds to pay for a ceremony every five years on 25th July, when two widows, a fiddler and ten girls under the age of fourteen would parade up to the monument. When there, they were to dance around it and sing the Hundredth Psalm. This parade – together with the traditional payment of £15 shared between the girls and £2 each to the widows – still takes place.*

Left: *The Water Tower, Trelissick, Cornwall. This water tower was originally built in 1860 to provide water to the main house on the Trelissick estate near Truro. It now has a new life as one of a number of National Trust properties that are available for holiday bookings. Note the squirrel on the weather-vane: the squirrel was the crest of the Gilbert family, who enlarged the house and landscaped the garden in which the tower is so prominent.*

Fort Putnam, Greystoke, Cumbria. The eleventh Duke of Norfolk, who lived at Greystoke Castle in the eighteenth century, supported the American colonies in the War of Independence and, to mark their victory, he built impressive fortifications on two of his farms – one called Bunkers Hill and the other Fort Putnam (seen here), named after Israel Putnam, an American general in the war.

The Barrow Monument, Ulverston, Cumbria. This tower, in the shape of a lighthouse, stands on Hoad Hill at Ulverston and commands fine views. It was built in 1850 to honour Sir John Barrow, born in the district in 1764, who was Secretary to the Admiralty for forty years and also helped to found the Royal Geographical Society.

PENZANCE. The Egyptian House (see opposite).

ST IVES. John Knill's Monument (see opposite).

TRELISSICK. The Water Tower (see opposite).

WERRINGTON. Three stone cones, known as the Sugar Loaves, on top of a seat in a deep round-arched recess, were built as an eyecatcher for Werrington Park *c.*1800.

CUMBRIA

GREYSTOKE. Fort Putnam (see above) and Bunkers Hill. The Duke also arranged for a third farm, now called Spire House, to be decorated with a spire.

KIRKBY LONSDALE. East of St Mary's parish church and overlooking the Lune valley stands the Gazebo, an eighteenth-century building erected in the former rectory garden.

MUNCASTER. In 1800 the first Lord Muncaster erected a large grey stone tower to commemorate the meeting in 1461 of the fugitive Henry VI and a local shepherd, who guided him to Muncaster Castle.

ULVERSTON. The Barrow Monument on Hoad Hill (see above).

Solomon's Temple, Buxton, Derbyshire. This 20 feet (6 metres) high battlemented tower was built in 1896 on Grinlow Barrow about two miles south of the spa town. Barbara Jones tells us that it gets its name from an earlier temple – 'built by public subscription to relieve unemployment' – on the same site on ground belonging to a farmer called Solomon Mycock.

DERBYSHIRE.

BUXTON. Solomon's Temple (see above).

CHATSWORTH. In the gardens of Chatsworth House, developed by 'Capability' Brown, Joseph Paxton and others, are Flora's Temple, a grotto, a maze, a summerhouse, an orangery and a magnificent cascade. Overlooking the house is the Hunting Tower (see below).

KEDLESTON. Kedleston Hall and the park were both created to Robert Adam's design between 1759 and 1776 and are now National Trust property. Enter by the arched gateway of North Lodge, cross the river by the three-arched bridge, which was built as an eyecatcher, and there is a combined boathouse and fishing pavilion to the west of it. Hidden in the trees to the north of the lake is a sulphur bath house, whilst in the garden there is an orangery together with a summerhouse.

The Hunting Tower in the grounds of Chatsworth House, Derbyshire, is less visited than the rest of the gardens because it stands on a hillside to the north-east of the house. From it there are fine views of the estate. It was built by Bess of Hardwick in 1582 as a prospect tower and Headley and Meulenkamp suggest that – as Freston Tower in Suffolk might be part of a demolished house – this is possibly the 'oldest free-standing, purpose-built folly tower in Britain'.

Riber Castle, Matlock, Derbyshire, sometimes known as Smedley's Folly, was built between 1862 and 1868 by John Smedley with stone from his own quarry and from Tansley quarries nearby. It was lavishly decorated inside and with full central heating, but Smedley lived only to 1874 to enjoy the fruits of his labours. After his widow died, the castle became a preparatory school but this closed in 1930 and, after remaining empty for many years, the building was demolished, except for the façade that overlooks Matlock.

MATLOCK. Riber Castle (see above).

MATLOCK BATH. A Victorian lookout tower was built by John Petchell on the Heights of Abraham above the town.

RENISHAW. At Renishaw Hall, the home of the Sitwell family, there are a round house or dairy, a Gothic temple (a ruined aviary), a *cottage orné* and the Gothic archway of 1805.

STANTON MOOR. The Reform Tower, standing on Stanton Moor Edge, between Rowsley and Birchover, was erected in 1832 to commemorate the passing of the Reform Act. The inscription reads 'Earl Grey 1832'.

SUDBURY. In the grounds of Sudbury Hall is an early folly, the Deerfold, built about 1723, with a sham gatehouse added in the early nineteenth century.

SWARKESTONE. The Swarkestone Pavilion, which has been restored by the Landmark Trust as a holiday home, was built originally in 1632 as a 'bowle alley house' by a mason, Richard Shepperd, although probably designed by John Smythson.

DEVON

BARNSTAPLE. Upcott Folly was built as an eyecatcher for Upcott House, some miles north of Barnstaple, and stands in a field on the Braunton road. The house dates from 1752 but this castellated sham gatehouse was built in the nineteenth century.

BRAUNTON. A tower was built by Thomas Mortimer in 1846 to celebrate the repeal of the Corn Laws.

Haldon Belvedere, Doddiscombsleigh, Devon, was built in 1788 by Sir Robert Palk in memory of his great friend Major-General Stringer Lawrence, and so it is also known as Lawrence Castle. The triangular tower, which stands 70 feet (21 metres) high, is situated 800 feet (240 metres) above sea level on the hills near Exeter. Since its restoration in 1995, it has been visible for miles in its white plaster coating.

Below: *A La Ronde, Exmouth, Devon, a sixteen-sided cottage orné, built by the Misses Jane and Mary Parminter in 1798. Now in the care of the National Trust, it has an octagonal hall and rooms leading off, filled with things which they made. The most exciting part of the house is the shell-encrusted gallery and the staircase leading up to it. Because the gallery is in a very fragile state, it is normally viewed by closed-circuit television.*

CHAGFORD. Rushford Tower at Rushford Barton, which was built in the nineteenth century for the Hayter Ames family of Chagford House, was featured in a 1984 BBC television production of R. F. Delderfield's *Diana*.

COMBE MARTIN. The Pack o' Cards is an inn, built early in the eighteenth century, which originally had fifty-two windows, thirteen doors on each floor and four floors.

DODDISCOMBSLEIGH. Haldon Belvedere (see opposite).

EXMOUTH. A La Ronde – a sixteen-sided *cottage orné* (see opposite).

FILLEIGH. When William Kent transformed the Castle Hill estate in 1730, he built a triumphal arch as an eyecatcher for the house. Here are also the Holwell Temple, a sham village tower, the Humpy Bridge, Nazareth (the menagerie), the Spar House, Sybil's Cave, the Sunrise Temple and the Ugly Bridge.

OFFWELL. Bishop Copplestone's Folly (see below).

POWDERHAM CASTLE. The Belvedere, very similar in shape to the Haldon Belvedere at Doddiscombsleigh, was built in 1773 and stands in the deer park of the Earls of Devon overlooking the river Exe.

Bishop Copplestone's Folly, Offwell, Devon. This 80 feet (24 metres) high tower was built by Edward Copplestone after he became Bishop of Llandaff in 1828. There are various explanations as to why the tower was built – some say that it is only a water tower – but the main one is that the Bishop, very reluctant to leave his home in Offwell, built this tower so that he could overlook his diocese in South Wales without the inconvenience of travel! As his flock was at least 50 miles away, with a range of hills between Offwell and Wales, the tower would have been quite useless for this purpose.

Grange Arch, Creech, Dorset, was built in 1746 by Denis Bond as an eyecatcher for Creech Grange. Standing on the crest of the Purbeck Hills, 3 miles west of Corfe Castle, it is built entirely of Portland stone, which has withstood the elements very well, and has been a National Trust property since 1942.

DORSET

CREECH. Grange Arch (see above).

HORTON. Sturt's Folly (see below).

KIMMERIDGE. Clavel Tower is situated on a cliff overlooking Kimmeridge Bay and within sight of the Grange Arch at Creech. The tower is three storeys high with an interesting quatrefoil balcony on the top and a Doric colonnade around the ground floor. It is in danger of collapsing over the cliff and there are plans to move it.

LULWORTH. Lulworth Castle was built as a hunting lodge in 1608 and, after a disastrous fire in 1929, has been fully restored. Also here are the so-called Clare Towers and unusual lodges restored by English Heritage.

MORDEN. The Gothic Tower in Charborough Park was built in 1790 and restored in 1839 after being struck by lightning.

PORTESHAM. The Hardy Monument was erected on Black Down to commemorate Admiral Sir Thomas Hardy, who lived in the local manor. He was on HMS *Victory* when Nelson was killed at Trafalgar.

Horton Tower, Horton, Dorset. This massive tower, also known as Sturt's Folly, stands back from the link road between the A354 near Gussage St Michael and the A31 a few miles south-west of Ringwood. The seven-storey, 120 feet (37 metres) high tower was built in 1722 by Humphrey Sturt, supposedly so that he could watch the deer on his estate, but apparently he never used it. The cock-fight scene in the film of Hardy's 'Far from the Madding Crowd' was filmed inside this tower.

The Deer House, Bishop Auckland, County Durham, in fine sham castle tradition, complete with tower, pinnacles and castellations, was built in Auckland Park in 1760 by Bishop Trevor to provide a winter refuge for deer in the outer cloister. It is now classified as an ancient monument and is accessible whenever the park is open.

DURHAM

BISHOP AUCKLAND. The Deer House (see above).

ROWLANDS GILL. The Column of British Liberty, Gibside (see below).

STAINDROP. The eyecatcher built on a hill behind Raby Castle consists of a long castellated façade with towers and walls on either side of an arch.

The Column of British Liberty, Gibside, County Durham. Just 5 miles to the south-east of Newcastle, the ornamental grounds at Gibside were created by George Bowes MP – one of the principal Durham coal owners – who spent some of his fortune in developing and landscaping Gibside in the 1740s and 1750s. Many of the buildings, unfortunately, were ruined over the years by mining subsidence and the hall was destroyed by fire in the 1920s. The 152 feet (46 metres) high Column of British Liberty, however, has stood its ground. It took seven years to build, between 1750 and 1757, and the statue of a woman on top was, apparently, carved in situ. The estate is now administered by the National Trust although the 1740 Banqueting House is leased to the Landmark Trust.

The Penshaw Monument, Washington, County Durham. Erected in 1844 as a memorial to John Lambton, first Earl of Durham and Governor-General of Canada, who died in 1840, the monument, a close copy of the Temple of Theseus in Athens, is 100 feet (30 metres) long, 53 feet (16 metres) wide and almost completely black with soot.

WASHINGTON. The Penshaw Monument (see above).

WESTERTON. A circular round tower, although known as Westerton Folly, was built as an observatory by Thomas Wright in 1750. He was born in the county and a plaque commemorating his work as a mathematician and astronomer was placed on the tower by Durham University in 1950.

ESSEX

AUDLEY END. The grounds at Audley End, near Saffron Walden, were landscaped by 'Capability' Brown in 1764, and embellished by Robert Adam with a Temple of Victory, a Temple of Concord, a three-arched bridge to the south-west and a miniature tea-pavilion on the Tea-House Bridge over the river Cam.

BRIGHTLINGSEA. Bateman's Folly is a concrete tower at the harbour.

COLCHESTER. There is an eighteenth-century arch in the grounds of the castle and a Gothic temple façade to a summerhouse in the garden of the Minories, the gallery and art museum across the road from Colchester Castle.

PENTLOW. The Bull Tower at Pentlow is 70 feet (21 metres) high and is in the garden of the former rectory. Although on private property, it can be clearly seen from the Long Melford to Clare road just across the border in Suffolk. It was built in 1859 by a dutiful son, Edward Bull, who placed a tablet over the door which reads: 'Erected to the memory of his honoured parents, the Rev. John Bull MA and Margaret his wife, on a spot they loved so well by Edward Bull MA 1859'.

GLOUCESTERSHIRE AND BRISTOL

BADMINTON. The Worcester Lodge, built by William Kent c.1740, is an eyecatcher to the house, and Thomas Wright was responsible for the Ragged Castle, at one time probably a keeper's lodge, the castellated farm buildings and the Hermit's Cell.

BERKELEY. In the grounds of Berkeley Castle the eighteenth-century castellated stables were built as an eyecatcher. About one mile to the south-west, in the middle of Whitcliff Park, is Park House, a square belvedere three storeys high, with an octagonal tower at each corner.

BRISLINGTON. The Black Castle or Arnos Castle was built by William Reeve, a local copper smelter. In the 1740s he built himself a Gothic house at Brislington and in 1750 he had stables and offices constructed in the form of a castle. With its turrets, keep and castellations, it was a very bold and striking building and was dubbed the 'Devil's Cathedral' by Horace Walpole in 1766. Today, however, after being used for many purposes, it is a private club.

Blaise Castle, Henbury, Bristol. This sham Castle stands on a hill in the grounds of Blaise House, now owned by Bristol City Council, between Avonmouth and Henbury. It was built in 1776 by Thomas Farr, a wealthy merchant, and, although the architect is unknown, it is possible that it was developed from a Sanderson Miller design.

CIRENCESTER. Though Cirencester House is not open to the public the park is, and Alfred's Hall, considered to be the first sham ruin, stands in the middle. It was created by the first Earl Bathurst with help from his friend Alexander Pope in 1721–33.

CLIFTON. Thomas Goldney (1696–1768) created on a hill at Clifton, overlooking Bristol, a fine garden in which he built a grotto, a Gothic summerhouse and a 'pretty' castellated round tower which supplied water to the grotto.

HENBURY. Blaise Castle (see above).

PAINSWICK. The Red House and other buildings can be seen in the restored Rococo Garden (see below).

The Red House, Painswick Rococo Garden, Gloucestershire. Painswick House and its stables were built by Charles Hyett towards the end of his life in 1735 but it was his son, Benjamin, who created the Rococo Garden and its various buildings in the 1740s. The garden stayed more or less unchanged until 1960, when it was abandoned. However, in 1984 restoration began, not only of the garden but also of the buildings, including the Doric Seat, the Eagle House, the Pigeon House, the Exedra and the Red House. The asymmetrical Red House has two façades directed respectively down the approach path and along the main vista. On the wall of the inner room is a plaster cast of the Hyett coat of arms.

RODBOROUGH. Rodborough Fort, south of Stroud, was built in 1761 by George Hawker as an eyecatcher. This substantial sham castle is some 600 feet (180 metres) above sea level. The building is in private hands.

STINCHCOMBE. In Stancombe Park, created *c.*1840, there are summerhouses, grottoes, pavilions, a temple and a square court with a massive keyhole gateway. The park is private but occasionally open in the summer.

HAMPSHIRE

EAGLEHURST. Luttrell's Tower (see below).

FARLEY DOWN. Farley Mount Pyramid (see opposite).

HAVANT. The Beacon, Staunton Country Park (see opposite).

HIGHCLERE. In the grounds of Highclere Castle, the seat of the Earls of Carnarvon, there are several follies, including Heaven's Gate, an eyecatcher arch built in 1731, and Jackdaw's Castle, built in 1743.

ODIHAM. King John's Hunting Lodge, built *c.*1740, is the only survivor of several follies built in Dogmersfield Park by Paulet St John, who also built the pyramid-shaped monument on Farley Down. The lodge stands by a small pond known as Wilkes's Water.

SWAY. Peterson's Tower (see opposite).

Luttrell's Tower at Eaglehurst, near Fawley in Hampshire, was built by Temple Simon Luttrell about 1780, to enable him to watch the ships on the Solent. Tradition maintains, however, that the tower later became a centre for smugglers. It was used by Marconi in the First World War for wireless experiments and it is now one of the Landmark Trust's holiday homes.

Left: *The Farley Down monument, at Farley Chamberlayne, Hampshire, is a 30 feet (9 metres) high pyramid on the downs south-east of Winchester, standing on the grave of a horse which saved the life of its owner. A tablet inside reads as follows: 'Underneath lies buried a horse the property of Paulet St John Esq. That in the month of September 1733, it leaped into a chalk pit 25 feet deep a foxhunting with his master on his back'. Both survived and the horse was subsequently renamed 'Beware Chalkpit'.*

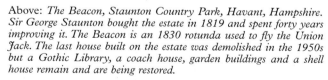

Above: *The Beacon, Staunton Country Park, Havant, Hampshire. Sir George Staunton bought the estate in 1819 and spent forty years improving it. The Beacon is an 1830 rotunda used to fly the Union Jack. The last house built on the estate was demolished in the 1950s but a Gothic Library, a coach house, garden buildings and a shell house remain and are being restored.*

Left: *Peterson's Tower, Sway, Hampshire. This handsome tower, 220 feet (67 metres) high, was built by Andrew Peterson, who had returned to England after retirement as a High Court judge in India in the late nineteenth century. It is said that he was inspired by the spirit of Christopher Wren to use concrete blocks, hitherto untried for building. Another story is that he wanted to introduce Hindu burial customs into England and that he wished to be entombed at the top. Whether or not there is any truth in either of these stories, the tower, which still stands on the edge of the New Forest, was built entirely without scaffolding and on its completion in 1885 was the first major building in Britain to be built from concrete.*

Shobdon Arches, Shobdon, Herefordshire. When the original Norman church at Shobdon was demolished – except for the tower – and rebuilt in a Gothic style by Viscount Bateman in 1756, these remains of the old church, comprising the chancel arch and two doorway arches, were re-erected in Shobdon Park as an eyecatcher. The columns and arches are decorated with ornate carvings but they have deteriorated badly after exposure to the elements for two and a half centuries. The church interior should not be missed.

HEREFORDSHIRE
SHOBDON. Shobdon Arches (see above).

HERTFORDSHIRE
AYOT ST LAWRENCE. In 1778 Sir Lionel Lyde built what is now called the 'New' church: the architect was Nicholas Revett, who specialised in the classical touch. He designed what is virtually a Greek temple to act as an eyecatcher to the manor. The Bishop of Lincoln prevented the complete destruction of the old church and

Folly Arch, Brookmans Park, Hertfordshire. The precise date of this folly is uncertain, but it is an early example of medieval revival from a design by James Gibbs and was erected on the Gobions estate by Sir Jeremy Sambrooke some time before his death in 1754. The arch, which is built entirely of bricks, is set back from the roadside at the junction of Swanley Bar Lane and Hawkshead Road, so it can be seen very easily. It is said that there is a farthing between each pair of bricks!

Stratton's Observatory, Little Berkhamsted, Hertfordshire. This castellated tower was built by Admiral John Stratton in 1789 and the traditional story is that he built the tower so that he could observe the movement of shipping on the River Thames from one of the top windows. Even though the tower is 92 feet (28 metres) high and 350 feet (106 metres) above sea level, this must have been quite impossible as it is at least 17 miles from the river, and it is much more likely that supply created a demand and that its construction helped to solve an unemployment problem. The tower was built from the bricks of an old ruined house nearby and 'Admirals do not care for untidiness and idle hands!'

so the building remains as a picturesque ruin.

BENINGTON. Now not much more than a hamlet on the edge of Stevenage, Benington has a long history and the present Lordship house was built in the eighteenth century on the site of a castle that was destroyed in 1212. The sham castle gatehouse was designed in 1832 by Pulham, a landscape gardener, and may be seen when the gardens are open to the public.

BROOKMANS PARK. Folly Arch (see opposite).

LITTLE BERKHAMSTED. Stratton's Observatory (see above).

ST PAUL'S WALDEN. The grounds of the The Bury were begun in 1720 by Edward Gilbert, an ancestor of the Bowes-Lyon family. They contain a domed temple, an octagonal garden house, a *cottage orné* and much statuary. Also, by the lake is a temple designed by Sir William Chambers in 1773, built originally in Kent and re-erected here in 1961.

TRING. The park, south of the bypass, has been leased by Dacorum Council to the Woodland Trust and contains a four-column Ionic summerhouse and an obelisk supposedly to the memory of Nell Gwynne.

WARE. Scott's Grotto is in Scott's Road. It was started in 1734 by Samuel Scott when his son, John, was only four years old but John Scott completed the scheme *c.*1770. After many years of neglect, it has now been restored and there are regular summer openings.

ISLE OF MAN

LANGNESS. Herring Tower (see right).

The Herring Tower, Langness, Isle of Man. Described originally as a 'daymark', that is 'a navigation reference point for sailors', the tower was built so that a beacon lit on top could guide home the herring fleet.

Yarborough Obelisk, Bembridge, Isle of Wight, was built in 1849, erected in memory of the Earl of Yarborough, who founded the Royal Yacht Squadron.

ISLE OF WIGHT
BEMBRIDGE. The Yarborough Obelisk (see left).

RYDE. The Appley Tower (see below).

KENT
BIRCHINGTON. The Waterloo Tower in Quex Park was built in the early nineteenth century by John Powell to house a peal of twelve bells. As well as the bells, the tower has the added attraction of a graceful cast-iron spire on top like a miniature Eiffel Tower.

COBHAM. At Cobham Hall, now a girls' school, near Rochester there is Wyatt's mausoleum for the Earl of Darnley, commissioned in 1783 but never consecrated. Here are also a Gothic pump-house, Repton's Seat, an aviary, Merlin's Grotto, the orangery, a rustic dairy and another of Sir William Chambers's Ionic temples.

HADLOW. May's Folly Tower (see opposite).

KINGSGATE. In the mid eighteenth century Lord Holland built a number of follies on his Kingsgate estate between Margate and Ramsgate. Many of these have been demolished or blown down, but the Hackemdown Clock Tower (in the grounds of the convent school at Port Regis) and Kingsgate Castle (now a hotel) are among those which have survived.

MARGATE. The Shell Grotto here was discovered in 1835 by a local man digging out a disused well. This shell-lined underground grotto is now open to the public.

Appley Tower, Ryde, Isle of Wight, was designed by Thomas Hellyer in the mid nineteenth century and stands at the eastern end of the promenade. Originally a prospect tower, it has been used as a gift shop and information point.

May's Folly Tower at Hadlow, Kent, was built by Walter May in 1840 to complete his Gothic Revival mansion but the tower is all that survives, and this has now been truncated, as shown in the 'before' and 'after' illustrations.

SEVENOAKS. The Bird House in Knole Park was built to house the collection of foreign birds owned by Lionel, first Duke of Dorset. It is now a private house.

SHEERNESS. The Ship on Shore Grotto owes its name to the Ship on Shore Inn, by which it stands. A ship loaded with cement in barrels was wrecked nearby *c.*1830 and, the cement having set, a farmer used the barrel blocks to build this folly.

LANCASHIRE

LANCASTER. The Ashton Memorial, built between 1907 and 1909, was commissioned by Lord Ashton as a monument to his family. Standing at the top of an elaborate staircase in Williamson Park, it is made of Portland stone and consists of coupled columns supporting a copper dome.

ORMSKIRK. The Sisters' Folly. The parish church has both a square tower and a tapering steeple: a popular, but unlikely, story explains this by saying that two sisters who were endowing the church in the fourteenth century could not agree whether it should have a tower or a spire, so they gave it both!

RIVINGTON. Rivington Pike Folly is a 20 feet (6 metres) high square stone tower on the Pennines between Chorley and Horwich. It was built as a shelter in the eighteenth century.

The Temple of Venus, Garendon Park, Loughborough, Leicestershire. Garendon Park lies between the M1 motorway and Loughborough University and its monuments, including the Triumphal Arch, the Temple of Venus and an 80 feet (24 metres) high obelisk, remain as a reminder of Ambrose Phillipps, who made the Grand Tour in the early eighteenth century and set about improving his estate in the then fashionable manner on his return. Phillipps unfortunately died in 1737, when he was only thirty years old, and his grand scheme was tragically curtailed. The park is not open to the public, although viewing arrangements can be made and the circular Temple of Venus, which is based on the Temple of Vista still preserved in Rome, can be seen from the road.

LEICESTERSHIRE

BELVOIR CASTLE. In the Spring Gardens are a circular thatched temple built at the beginning of the nineteenth century and known as the Moss House, a grotto and a mausoleum. The hound kennels and the dairy resulted from the collaboration between James Wyatt and the fifth Duchess of Rutland in 1801–13.

LOUGHBOROUGH. The Temple of Venus in the private grounds of Garendon Park (see above).

NEWTOWN LINFORD. Old John Folly in Bradgate Park (see below).

Old John Folly, Bradgate Park, Newtown Linford, Leicestershire. This mock ruin and supporting arch, standing in a prominent position, can be reached from all parts of Bradgate Park, a public space to the north-east of Leicester. Little is known about its origins – except the date of 1786 – although it is believed that it was erected by the Earl of Stamford to the memory of Old John, one of his retainers, who was accidentally killed on the spot when a flagpole fell on him during bonfire celebrations to mark the coming of age of the Earl's eldest son. There is, however, no proof of this story and, as Old John was a miller, perhaps when the mill was demolished the mock ruin was put up as an eye-catcher on the same spot.

Bellmount Tower, Belton, Lincolnshire, known locally as 'Lord Brownlow's Breeches' and designed by William Eames in 1749, is more an arch than a tower and was built originally as a hunting lodge. A few years after acquiring the Belton estate – when the tower was virtually derelict – the National Trust, with the help of a substantial grant from English Heritage, completely restored it and since 1990 there has been unlimited access to the site of the tower, which stands nearly 2 miles from the hall at the end of an avenue of trees. On certain days in the summer, the tower itself is open and it is possible to climb up to the single room above the arch.

LINCOLNSHIRE

BELTON. Bellmount Tower (see above).

BROCKLESBY. The mausoleum was built by James Wyatt (considered his masterpiece) in 1787–92 in memory of Sophia Pelham, wife of the first Lord Yarborough. Also at Brocklesby are kennels, a root house, Arabella's Temple, a seven-arched bridge and a memorial arch.

COLEBY. In the grounds of Coleby Hall, 7 miles due south of Lincoln, there is a temple to Pitt, designed by the then owner, Thomas Scrope. In 1762 he commissioned Sir William Chambers to design the Temple of Romulus and Remus and, later, an imitation Roman gateway, which is a copy of the Newport Arch in Lincoln.

DUNSTON. In 1751 Dunston, a village to the south-east of Lincoln, was a very remote place indeed. Sir Francis Dashwood (of West Wycombe), who had inherited the property through his wife, erected a pillar complete with lanterns to guide travellers. A statue of George III replaced the lanterns in 1810 but was removed in the Second World War because it was a danger to aircraft.

EAGLE. The Jungle at Eagle Moor is a farmhouse of burnt bricks with a roughly castellated front, curious ogee windows and round tower-like ends. Built originally in early nineteenth century to house a zoo – hence the name – it has been extensively modernised behind the façade. It is not accessible to the public but the folly front can be seen from the minor road between Eagle and Harby.

FILLINGHAM. Ermine Lodge Gateway, with triangular lodges on either side, situated on the B1398, was built *c.*1760 and is one of the two Gothic archways to Summer Castle, which was built for Sir Cecil Wray. A seventeenth-century cottage, known as The Manor House, is in the grounds and acts as an eyecatcher.

HOLYWELL. At Holywell Hall, near the Rutland border, there are a fishing temple, an orangery, a balustrated bridge and, right on the lawn as a 'garden ornament', the eighteenth-century St Wilfrid's church decorated with a medley of fragments from various centuries.

SWINSTEAD. The Vanbrugh Pavilion. In 1722 Sir John Vanbrugh was commissioned by the first Earl of Ancaster to rebuild the old Grimsthorpe Castle and, although evidence is confusing, this summerhouse on the edge of Swinstead is unmistakably by Vanbrugh and very similar to his Belvedere at Claremont in Surrey. After many years of neglect, it was restored in 1992 and is now a private house.

LONDON AND MIDDLESEX

BAYSWATER. Numbers 23 and 24 Leinster Gardens are sham façades of houses, put up to preserve the appearance of the road after the originals were pulled down when the Metropolitan Railway was extended in 1868.

GUNNERSBURY PARK, W3. Princess Amelia, daughter of George II, lived on the estate between 1761 and 1786 and built a number of follies. These have disappeared, except for the Doric temple-cum-dairy. A century later, in 1860, a castellated octagonal tower – a 'building deliberately ruinous' – was added near the Potomac Pond close to the elevated section of the M4 motorway.

KEW. The Pagoda in Kew Gardens (see below).

SHOOTER'S HILL. Severndroog Castle – which is actually a triangular tower and

not a castle at all – was built in 1784 in Castlewood Park, at Shooter's Hill, SE18, and was featured in a BBC *Restoration* programme. It was built to celebrate the exploits of Sir William James and in particular the capture of the real Severndroog Castle on the coast of Malabar in India in 1760.

The Pagoda, Kew Gardens, London. The Pagoda was built by Sir William Chambers for Augusta, Dowager Princess of Wales, in 1761. The ten-storey building is 163 feet (50 metres) high and, above the lowest storey, each storey decreases by one foot in diameter and one in height from the next storey below. The Pagoda is not open to the public because of the narrowness of the staircase but, after 250 years, remains a great London landmark. There are other buildings by Chambers in the gardens.

SOHO, W1. The octagonal summerhouse in the middle of Soho Square is used by gardeners for their tools but its original purpose is unknown.

STRAWBERRY HILL. Horace Walpole's Gothic house is now part of St Mary's Teacher Training College and is not open to the public. Walpole built a number of garden buildings but the only survivor is his Chapel in the Woods, which has been restored by the college.

TWICKENHAM. Pope's Grotto, constructed early in the eighteenth century, was probably one of the first in England. It is in the grounds of St Catherine's Convent School for girls and may be viewed by appointment with the School Secretary.

NORFOLK

BLICKLING. The Racecourse Stand (see below).

BRININGHAM. Belle Vue Tower stands in a field off the B1354. Originally a beacon tower built in the sixteenth century, it became an observatory in the eighteenth century and was used in both World Wars as a signalling tower.

GUNTON PARK. The Hall was converted into houses and cottages by Kit Martin in the last two decades of the twentieth century, but the crowning glory of the scheme is the restoration of the 100 foot (30 metre) tower which is a lodge at the north end of the park. It was built in *c.*1829 by the third Lord Suffield when he was engaged in increasing the size of the park.

HOLKHAM. In the grounds of this fine Palladian mansion are an obelisk, a temple and a triumphal arch. The house and grounds are open to the public.

MELTON CONSTABLE. Called a 'sham castle bath house' by Barbara Jones and a 'menagerie' by Nikolaus Pevsner, a castellated building here was built to look like a church as an eyecatcher for Melton Hall.

SHERINGHAM. In Sheringham Park, administered by the National Trust, there is a temple designed by Humphry Repton in 1812 and finally built in 1975!

The Racecourse Stand, Blickling, Norfolk. In the grounds of Blickling Hall – now owned by the National Trust – are an orangery, a temple and a pyramid-shaped mausoleum of 1793. About a mile from the main gates is a square, castellated tower, with a round stair turret, called the Racecourse Stand. Built in 1773, it is now a private house, and the designer is unknown.

NORTHAMPTONSHIRE

ALTHORP. In the grounds of the Spencer estate there is a wooden temple by the lake: it is now a shrine to Diana, Princess of Wales, who lies buried on an island in the lake. Further out is the curious structure called The Standing or Falconry, dated 1611.

BOUGHTON. At Boughton Park there are the Hawking Tower (see below), the Spectacles (see opposite), together with Holly Lodge and Bunkers Hill Farm.

CASTLE ASHBY. A temple, a temple-fronted dairy, an aviary and a bridge are all attributed to 'Capability' Brown *c*.1761–7, while the orangery dates only from the middle of the nineteenth century.

FINEDON. On the Thrapston road, 2 miles to the east of the village, stands the Wellington Tower (see opposite). In the middle of the nineteenth century Squire William Mackworth-Dolben began to decorate ironstone buildings in the Finedon area with a variety of architectural novelties. Many houses still bear evidence of his efforts, although what was called the Volta Tower – built in memory of a son lost at sea – collapsed in 1951. A converted tower mill, visible from the Burton Latimer road and cleverly named Exmill Cottage, is topped by an embattled parapet, thus transforming it into an economical sham castle.

HORTON. Horton Hall was demolished in 1936 but in the grounds are lodges, one called The Arches, which was built as an eyecatcher for the second Earl of Halifax, and Thomas Wright's Menagerie of *c*.1750, which has been painstakingly restored.

LYVEDEN NEW BIELD. See page 6.

RUSHTON. The Triangular Lodge (see page 6).

The Hawking Tower, Boughton, Northamptonshire. The A508 Market Harborough to Northampton road passes the outskirts of Boughton village, where, in the eighteenth century, William Wentworth, the second Earl of Strafford, put up several follies in Boughton Park. The main gate lodge, known as the Hawking Tower – basically a copy of Steeple Lodge at his other estate, Wentworth Castle in Yorkshire – was built c.1770 to resemble a church tower. The ground and first floors are inhabited but the top room is bricked up although there is an outside stairway up to it.

The Spectacles, Boughton, Northamptonshire. Among the follies in Boughton Park is the Spectacles, which dates from about the same time as the Hawking Tower. This and other follies, such as Newpark Barn and Holly Lodge, show similarities to those at Wentworth.

The Wellington Tower, Finedon, Northamptonshire. The Duke of Wellington, when staying with his friend General Arbuthnot, thought that the local terrain, viewed from where the tower now stands, looked remarkably like the area around Waterloo and he explained the battle in terms of local landmarks. The tower was built about 1820 to commemorate both the battle and the Duke's visit.

NORTHUMBERLAND

ALNWICK. Brislaw or Brizlee Tower, 2 miles from the castle on a hill above the town, was designed by Robert Adam for the first Duke of Northumberland. Adam also designed the Ratcheugh Observatory, which stands even further away from the castle on the opposite side, as a 'ruin' to be an eyecatcher.

WALLINGTON HALL. At this National Trust property half a mile south of Cambo village can be seen four stone dragons' heads on the lawn. They were placed here in 1928 but were originally at the sham castle known as Rothley Castle built in the 1740s on a hilltop some 4 miles to the north-east. A short distance further north is Codger's Fort, built as a 'defence against the Scots' in 1745 and designed by Thomas Wright. Both these follies were designed as eyecatchers to Wallington Hall and the remains are now freely accessible from B6342, the road to Rothbury from Cambo.

WHITTON. Sharpe's Folly is a battlemented tower put up by Dr Sharpe in 1720, when he was vicar of nearby Rothbury, to provide work for the unemployed.

NOTTINGHAMSHIRE

NEWSTEAD ABBEY. Two sham forts were built by the fifth Lord Byron in the eighteenth century. The grounds of the abbey are open all the year round. One fort, which is now a private residence, can be viewed from the outside but the other, across the lake, is not accessible to the public.

The Sham Fort, Newstead Abbey, Nottinghamshire. William, fifth Baron Byron, the so-called 'wicked lord' and a great-uncle of the poet, had been in the Navy as a junior officer before inheriting the title and he built up a miniature navy on the estate lake. About 1760 he built two 'forts' fitted with cannons, one on each side of the lake, with the dual purpose of providing suitable grandstands from which he could conduct his naval battles and to serve as hides from which his guests could shoot duck on the lake. The larger of these forts is now a private residence but it is best seen from the other side of the lake.

Lord Berners's Folly, Faringdon, Oxfordshire, was the last true folly to be built but its construction in 1935 was authorised only after many objections had been overcome. The 140 foot (43 metre) tower, standing among trees in a field to the east of the town, is square apart from a small octagonal upper section with pinnacles.

OXFORDSHIRE

BLENHEIM PALACE. Among the trees to the south-east of the Water Gardens are three small temples, all surrounded by iron railings: the Temple of Diana and a bridge, both by Sir William Chambers in 1773; the Temple of Health (to celebrate the recovery of George III from illness in 1789); and another temple with an added dedication to Sir Winston Churchill, who was born at Blenheim.

COLESHILL. Strattenborough Castle is a farmhouse, the rear of which was disguised by turrets and battlements in 1792 to provide an eyecatcher from Coleshill House, which was burnt down in the 1950s.

FARINGDON. Lord Berners's Folly (see right).

STEEPLE ASTON. The Rousham Eyecatcher (see below).

WHEATLEY. The sham Gothic temple at Shotover House, a few miles east of Oxford, terminates the canal and acts as an eyecatcher from the house. The grounds also contain an obelisk and an octagonal temple designed by William Kent.

WROXTON. The Gothic archway at Drayton, built about 1750, was designed as part of the landscaping of the Wroxton estate – probably by Sanderson Miller. Nearer to the house are an obelisk and a small temple.

The Rousham Eyecatcher, Steeple Aston, Oxfordshire. William Kent redesigned the gardens at Rousham House in 1738 and, unlike so many other designs of the eighteenth century, they remain almost as planned. To complete his scheme, Kent transformed a former watermill into the Chapel of the Mill and built the Rousham Eyecatcher. This folly is more a screen than a sham castle, but it is one of the earliest sham ruins. It stands in a field a mile or two from the house, from where it is best viewed. It is visible from the road between Hopcrofts Holt and Lower Heyford, but a closer view is possible from a track leading out of the village of Steeple Aston.

Fort Henry, Exton Park, Rutland. 2 miles from Exton Hall, the home of the Noel family, is Fort Henry, a pretty summerhouse or pavilion which stands immediately beside the large ornamental lake. Although it is not open to the public, except on special occasions, it is an elegant example of late-eighteenth-century Gothic. Like Lord Byron at Newstead Abbey in Nottinghamshire, Henry Noel, the sixth Earl of Gainsborough, who died in 1798, enjoyed re-enacting the great sea battles of his time on the lake and Fort Henry would, no doubt, have made a fine grandstand for these battles between miniature men-of-war crewed by his tenants and servants.

The Pinnacled Dovecote, Exton Park, Rutland, is in another part of the park, much nearer to the church and to the present hall, which was built in 1850. The dovecote is surrounded by a livestock shelter and is near another, much smaller stretch of water. Built about the same time as Fort Henry, a time when pigeons were no longer in demand for the winter diet, it is more likely to have been intended as an eyecatcher seen from the old hall, which was burnt down in 1810.

The Egyptian Aviary, Tong, Shropshire. Various follies were built by George Durant between 1815 and 1840 but all have been swept away except a lodge and what is called the Egyptian Aviary, an elaborate pyramidal henhouse at Vauxhall Farm across the park.

RUTLAND

EXTON. In different parts of Exton Park are Fort Henry and a pinnacled dovecote (see opposite page for both).

SHROPSHIRE

TONG. The Egyptian Aviary (see right).

WESTON-UNDER-REDCASTLE. After a hundred years of neglect, Hawkstone Park, created in the eighteenth century by Sir Rowland Hill, has been restored and is now open to the public. Here are intricate pathways, caves, arches, bridges, a hermitage and a grotto, together with various follies including the White Tower and the Red Castle.

SOMERSET

BANWELL. On the A371 east of Weston-super-Mare are Bishop Law's Tower and a number of caves which the Bishop 'improved' from 1830 onwards.

BATH. Ralph Allen's Sham Castle (see below).

Ralph Allen's Sham Castle, Bath, Somerset. This sham castle was designed by Sanderson Miller, who was commissioned by Ralph Allen to 'improve the view' after the Palladian-style Prior Park had been built for him by John Wood. Miller designed the castle, of local stone, in 1762 and it is not only an eyecatcher for Prior Park but, because of its commanding position, is visible from all over the city.

BRUTON. The Towers is an archway on the minor road between Redlynch and Shepton Montague. It was intended to front a new road to Redlynch Park but the road was never built.

CURRY RIVEL. The Burton Pynsent Column was erected in 1765 as a memorial to Sir William Pynsent, the last of his line, who bequeathed his Burton estate to William Pitt, the Earl of Chatham. It contains a spiral staircase but the entrance to the column has now been blocked up after a cow fell to its death after, apparently, climbing up to the top!

DUNSTER. Conygar Hill Tower, overlooking the village, looks like an outpost of the castle but was built in 1775 as a prospect tower.

EAST CRANMORE. Cranmore Tower, on the A361 between Frome and Shepton Mallet, stands 900 feet (275 metres) above sea level on the Mendips and commands fine views. It was built by a Mr Paget in 1862.

GOATHURST. Halswell House has a collection of eighteenth-century follies, which, after many years of neglect, are being gradually restored. The Somerset Buildings Preservation Trust has taken over the care of most of the buildings, including the Ionic Temple of Harmony, a Doric rotunda (under which there is an icehouse), the Temple of Pan and 'Robin Hood's Hut', which is fully restored and now administered by the Landmark Trust.

MONTACUTE. The tower standing on top of St Michael's Hill – called the Phelps Observation Folly in the National Trust guide – can be clearly seen from Montacute House and there is a marked pathway up to it.

WESTON-IN-GORDANO. Walton Castle stands on Castle Hill by the golf course between Clevedon and Weston-in-Gordano, and mystery surrounds its origins. The Ordnance map shows it as 'remains of castle' although there is no evidence to prove that there ever was a real castle on the site and no firmer date can be given for this building than the early eighteenth century. It is now a private house.

YEOVIL. The Barwick Park follies (see below).

Jack the Treacle Eater, Barwick Park, near Yeovil, Somerset. Four follies were built by George Messiter in Barwick Park, just south of Yeovil, in order to mark the park boundaries. Research by Barbara Jones has shown that they were most likely built c.1770. They are the Fish Tower, the Obelisk, the Cone and the most spectacular, 'Jack the Treacle Eater', which stands, protected by a trench, on the edge of the grounds of Barwick House. This folly can be reached on foot down a narrow track leading off a minor road from the A37 and South Somerset District Council has produced a very useful 'Follies Walk' pamphlet showing the way. The traditional story about Jack, who is commemorated by the figure on the top, is that he was a noted local runner who trained on treacle!

The Duck Tower, Alton Towers, Staffordshire. Sometimes called the Chinese Temple, this structure is actually a three-storeyed pagoda, which was designed by Robert Abraham and completed in 1827. It was based on the To-Ho Pagoda in Canton.

STAFFORDSHIRE

ALTON. Prominent features at Alton Towers (10 miles east of Stoke-on-Trent and quite separate from the Leisure Park) are the valley gardens created in the early nineteenth century. Here are a pagoda called the Duck Tower (see right), the Corkscrew Fountain, a Gothic prospect tower and what is known as the Druid's Sideboard – a miniature Stonehenge.

BIDDULPH. Chinese Bridge and Temple (see below).

The Chinese Bridge and Temple, Biddulph, Staffordshire. James Bateman, whose grandfather had made the family fortune from interests in iron, engineering and banking, built Biddulph Grange in 1842. He was a determined plant collector and, together with his friend Edward Cooke, spent twenty years developing the garden and stocking it with plants from all over the world. To set off the collection, they built several folly features including the Egyptian Court, the Cheshire Cottage and, most attractively, the Chinese Bridge and Temple. After the house and garden were occupied by an orthopaedic hospital the grounds became very neglected but have since been restored by the National Trust and are open to the public.

The Triumphal Arch, Shugborough Park, Staffordshire. In the middle of the eighteenth century, Admiral Anson's successful voyage around the world enabled him to enrich his country estate at Shugborough, near Stafford, with a variety of ornaments and follies. The Triumphal Arch, standing just above a railway line on the edge of the estate, is a reproduction of the Arch of Hadrian at Athens and is one of several fine buildings, including the Doric Temple, the Temple of the Winds, the Shepherd's Monument and the Lanthorn of Demosthenes.

CODSALL WOOD. The sham classical façade on Whitehouse Farm, built in 1725 by Francis Smith of Warwick, was originally put up to hide the farm from Chillington Hall and is considered to be the first eyecatcher of its kind. Chillington Hall's grounds are open on certain days.

CONSALL. At Consall Hall, near Stoke-on-Trent, in his own private landscape garden, William Podmore is building up a modern collection of follies: here you will find a Laund Pool, belvedere, summerhouse, pergola, Moon Dell and grotto, stone circle, Italian mock ruin and, in time, much more.

ENVILLE. Enville Hall is off the Stourbridge to Bridgnorth road and in the grounds a number of garden buildings were erected in the eighteenth century; some have been destroyed but steps have been taken to restore others, one being the Museum, which used to be the billiard room or the summerhouse. Another is the Gothic Gateway, an eyecatcher, probably designed by Sanderson Miller, comprising three arches, one of them open and fitted with a portcullis.

SHUGBOROUGH, Milford. Triumphal Arch, Shugborough Park (see above).

WESTON-UNDER-LIZARD. In Weston Park (which is sometimes shown as in Shropshire but is actually in Staffordshire), there are the Tower, a Temple of Diana, a

Woodbridge Lodge, Rendlesham, Suffolk. Rendlesham Hall no longer exists, but this lodge still stands just off the Eyke to Tunstall road. Built some time between 1790 and 1820 in the style of a Gothic chapter house, it is a single-storey building with three wings leading from it. Pinnacles abound and three flying buttresses join to support not another pinnacle but a chimney. The estate originally had five lodges, all of which remain in some form or another, but Woodbridge Lodge is the only one to survive in such a picturesque state.

pink cottage and a boat-house, all built in the eighteenth century. In 1992 these buildings were offered for sale or lease on the condition that they were restored.

SUFFOLK

EUSTON. Euston Mill, an eighteenth-century watermill disguised as a church, stands on the banks of the Little Ouse. It can be seen on the approach to Euston Hall, where in the grounds is a temple designed by William Kent in 1746.

FRESTON. The Freston Tower (see page 4).

RENDLESHAM. Woodbridge Lodge (see opposite).

TATTINGSTONE. The Tattingstone Wonder, near Ipswich, can be seen by making a diversion through the village off the A137 (see page 1).

THORPENESS. The House in the Clouds (see below).

The House in the Clouds, Thorpeness, Suffolk. G. Stuart Ogilvie, who inherited the estate in 1903, planned a holiday centre at the village of Thorpe before the First World War, but it was not until 1922 that his dream became a reality and was named Thorpeness. To provide water for the centre, he built a water tower that would be a visual asset. The tower was constructed and the tank itself was clad in weatherboard and provided with a steeply pitched roof, tall chimneys and mock windows. The lower part became living accommodation. Ogilvie then moved a post mill from his property at Aldringham and re-sited it to pump water up to the tank. When in 1963 the village was connected to the mains water supply, the tank became redundant and the tower became a family home.

The Belvedere, Claremont, Esher, Surrey. One part of the Claremont estate, not accessible to the public, is occupied by Claremont School but the landscape garden, which dates from the reign of Queen Anne, is now open to the public after restoration by the National Trust. It is one of the earliest of its kind to have survived. Kent, Bridgeman and 'Capability' Brown all had a hand in designing features at different periods – including the Grotto, the Island Pavilion and the Amphitheatre – but it was Sir John Vanbrugh who built a house here in the early part of the eighteenth century and, in 1717, the splendid brick Belvedere. It stands on a hillock, which used to be called The Mount, near to the present building (now the school). The Belvedere and the house belong to the school but the governors have allowed the National Trust to re-open the present view of the Belvedere, the oldest feature in the garden.

SURREY

BOX HILL. The flint circular tower on Box Hill above Dorking was built by Thomas Broadwood.

COBHAM. One mile to the east of Cobham is Painshill Park, which re-opened in 1989 after being magnificently restored by the Painshill Park Trust. The Honourable Charles Hamilton began building his follies about 1740 and they include the elegant Gothick Temple, a four-tiered Gothic tower, a grotto, a mausoleum, a Temple of Bacchus, a ruined abbey by the artificial lake and a

Turkish tent, which has been re-created in glass-fibre.

ESHER. The Belvedere, Claremont Landscape Garden (see above).

GODALMING. Along with the ornamental waterfowl at Busbridge Lakes is a romantic garden, landscaped in the middle of the eighteenth century and with a number of follies: the Hermit's Cave and icehouse, a Roman Doric temple, below which is a

Leptis Magna columns, Virginia Water, Surrey. These Roman columns, arches and odd pieces of stone were brought to England from North Africa in 1821, apparently as a gift from the Bey of Tripoli. They were first kept at the British Museum, but George IV had them brought to Virginia Water and arranged for Sir Jeffry Wyattville to re-erect them to form picturesque ruins by the lake. The site is near the Wheatsheaf Hotel at the south-east corner of Windsor Great Park.

grotto with the date '1810' on the wall inside, two rustic bridges and a pedimented Gothic boat-house.

LEITH HILL. Named after its builder, Richard Hull, a tower was built in 1764 on Leith Hill, the highest point in south-east England, several miles south-west of Dorking. The top of the hill is 965 feet (294 metres) above sea level and the tower was constructed to reach exactly 1000 feet.

VIRGINIA WATER. Leptis Magna columns (see opposite).

SUSSEX, EAST

BRIGHTLING. Mad Jack Fuller's follies (see below).

BRIGHTON. The Royal Pavilion of George IV (see below).

Mad Jack Fuller's follies, Brightling, East Sussex. Jack Fuller, the squire of Brightling Park, laid bets with his guests one evening that the spire of Dallington church could be seen from his house. Next morning he found that a small ridge had proved him wrong. It is not known whether he paid his debts but he built a cone 40 feet (12 metres) high, a sham spire representing the top of Dallington church, near Woods Corner on the B2096, where it could be seen from his dining-room. It is locally called the Sugar Loaf (above left). Jack Fuller built other follies, including an obelisk called the Needle, an observatory, a rotunda and, in 1810, twenty years before he died, a pyramid-shaped tomb for himself in Brightling churchyard (above right).

The Royal Pavilion, Brighton. In 1786 the Prince Regent (later George IV) took a house in what was then the fishing village of Brighton and, over the next thirty-five years, had it transformed by several architects into the Royal Pavilion. John Nash, who was hired in 1815 to 'Indianise' the already much enlarged house, added the domes and minarets, thus creating what Nigel Nicolson called 'Coleridge's pleasure-dome translated from Xanadu to an English seaside resort!'

ERIDGE. 3 miles south of Tunbridge Wells, Saxonbury Tower on Saxonbury Hill is a round brick tower built *c.*1820. It has been restored and is now a transmitting tower for a telephone company.

FIRLE. The castellated circular Firle Tower was built in 1822 on an eminence in Firle Park by Lord Gage. It was built as a gamekeeper's cottage so that he or Lord Gage himself could send signals to his deer-keeper at Ringmer, 7 miles away.

HEATHFIELD. The Gibraltar Tower, to the north-east of the village off the A265, in the north-west corner of Heathfield Park, was erected by Francis Newbery to commemorate the heroism of Lord Heathfield in the siege of Gibraltar in 1779.

SUSSEX, WEST

CLAYTON. The Gothic tunnel entrance on the London to Brighton railway line can be seen from the A273 opposite the fork road to Ditchling.

GOODWOOD. In the grounds of Goodwood House there is an elegant banqueting house, known as Carne's Seat, built *c.*1743 for the second Duke of Richmond. There is also a shell temple or grotto, which was begun in 1739 by Sarah, his wife. It has been carefully restored by Diana Reynell.

PULBOROUGH. Toat Monument is a six-sided tower erected in the 1820s at Toat Farm to mark the spot where Samuel Drinkald fell from his horse and was killed. Access is difficult but the monument can be seen across the fields.

RACTON. Racton Tower, built by Lord Halifax in 1772, is in Stanstead Park, near Rowland's Castle. This impressive tower, standing on a low hill, can be seen from the road near Rowland's Castle, due north of Emsworth.

SLINDON. The Nore Folly (see below).

SOUTH HARTING. The Vandalian Tower was built in the grounds of Uppark House in 1774 to commemorate not only the twenty-first birthday of Sir Harry Featherstonhaugh, but also the launching of a scheme to found a new American colony to be called 'Vandalia'. Little remains of it now but Uppark House, after a disastrous fire in 1989, has been completely rebuilt by the National Trust.

Nore Folly, Slindon, West Sussex, stands on the edge of a high beechwood. Built in the eighteenth century of flint with arches and a turret, it was restored by the National Trust in 1993 and is easily accessible.

Radway Tower, Edgehill, Warwickshire. Sanderson Miller inherited Radway Grange from his father in 1737, when he was only twenty, and soon began improving the grounds. He built his first Gothic building, the Thatched Cottage ('Egge Cottage'), in 1744 and between 1747 and 1750 he built his own mock castle, Radway Tower, on what is reputed to be the exact location where Charles I rallied his army before the battle of Edgehill in the Civil War. It is 6 miles north-west of Banbury and survives as part of the Castle Inn. Miller's reputation as a designer brought him commissions for similar towers on other estates.

WARWICKSHIRE

EDGBASTON. Built in 1758, Perrott's Folly, in Waterworks Lane, has been hailed as 'Birmingham's most eccentric building' and has been extensively restored. The building is said to be the inspiration for Tolkien's *Two Towers*.

RADWAY. Radway Tower, Edgehill (see right).

WILTSHIRE

AMESBURY. The Chinese House, a restored pavilion at Amesbury Abbey, is known to have existed in 1748 although it was probably rebuilt by Sir William Chambers in 1772.

FONTHILL GIFFORD. Some fragments remain of William Beckford's ill-fated mansion.

STOURHEAD. The Temple of Apollo (see page 3) and other garden buildings adorn the grounds of Henry Hoare's estate. On the perimeter is Alfred's Tower (see right).

TOLLARD ROYAL. Right on the border of Dorset and Wiltshire, the Larmer Tree Gardens were created by General Augustus Lane-Fox Pitt-Rivers between 1880 and 1890. Musical and other events take place here during the summer months in the Singing Theatre and there are also the Temple, the Indian House, the General's Room and, of course, the gardens themselves.

WHITEPARISH. The Pepperbox or Eyre's Folly (see page 7).

WILTON. In the grounds of Wilton House, the seat of the Earls of Pembroke and itself partly a creation of Inigo Jones, stand a number of buildings by well-known architects.

Alfred's Tower, Stourhead, Wiltshire. Alfred's Tower was built on Kingsettle Hill, 2 miles north-west of Stourhead House and on the perimeter of the gardens. This triangular tower was designed in 1765 by Henry Flitcroft, the designer of the Temple of Apollo and other buildings in the gardens, but it was not completed until 1772, after his death. Visible for miles around, it stands 160 feet (49 metres) high and was built, apparently, for three purposes: to celebrate King Alfred's victory over the Danes, the British victory over the French and the monarchy of King George III.

The Panorama Tower, Croome Park, Worcestershire. Croome was 'Capability' Brown's first complete landscape and not only made his reputation but influenced a new style of landscape design that was adopted over the next fifty years or more. Brown is also credited with building the house but Robert Adam was responsible for the various buildings in the park including the orangery, the Temple Greenhouse, the Owl House, a grotto and the rotunda. Since the Second World War, the house has been, at different times, a school, a conference centre and the home of a religious sect and the garden buildings were more or less neglected. In 1996, however, the National Trust acquired 670 acres (370 hectares) of the park and embarked on a ten-year restoration project. The Panorama Tower is another of Adam's follies but, although it is part of the estate, it stands in a field on the other side of the M5 motorway.

James Wyatt reassembled carvings which used to be on a grotto as a façade on a pavilion known as the Old Schoolhouse, and he was also responsible for placing the Holbein Porch, a piece of the original sixteenth-century house, at the end of a garden walk *c.*1805. The Casino of *c.*1750 is another of Chambers's designs and the famous Palladian Bridge was built in 1737.

WORCESTERSHIRE

BREDON. Parson's Folly is a square lookout tower on Bredon Hill, put up by Mr Parson at the end of the eighteenth century.

BROADWAY. The Broadway Tower (see page 9).

CROOME PARK. The Panorama Tower and other follies (see above).

DEFFORD. Dunstall Castle (see below).

HAGLEY. Hagley Hall and what Horace Walpole called the 'Ruinated Castle' of 1749 were both designed by Sanderson Miller. The Doric Temple of Theseus, designed by James ('Athenian') Stuart in 1758, was the first neo-classical building of its kind in England.

HALESOWEN. William Shenstone's 'Writing House', in a ruined state, is all that remains of a number of follies built *c.*1750 when he lived at The Leasowes.

ROUS LENCH. In 1890 Dr Chaffy, the local parson squire, not only built the village school and two outsized, half-timbered pillar-boxes for the village (and also for Radford) but also erected a 60 foot (19 metre) tower, modelled on an Italian campanile, in his own garden.

Dunstall Castle, Defford, Worcestershire. This massive sham castle stands right beside the road on Dunstall Common at Defford, southwest of Pershore, and consists of three tall towers, two round and the other one square, which are joined by two hollow walls, each pierced with a round-headed arch. Although it is within sight of Croome Park, opinion differs as to whether it was built as one of the Croome group and there is also mystery as to the builder: Headley, however, confidently states that it was built by Sanderson Miller.

YORKSHIRE, EAST

CARNABY. Supposed to have been modelled on the Temple of the Winds in Athens, the Carnaby Temple was built for Sir George Strickland *c.*1760. It is a three-storey, red-brick, octagonal tower with a brick lantern, arched and roofed and topped by a ball.

SLEDMERE. Castle Farm is a fortified structure built for Sir Christopher Sykes at the end of the eighteenth century in the grounds of Sledmere House, 8 miles north-east of Driffield. Although originally intended as a dower house, this eyecatcher and focal point for 'Capability' Brown's landscaped park was never used as such because it was too cold!

YORKSHIRE, NORTH

ASKE HALL. Between Richmond and Gilling, a mid-eighteenth-century sham castle in the grounds of the hall is called the Temple. One of the largest follies, it is a complex of Gothic arches, square and octagonal towers, with an isolated turret chamber. In the same area there was an outpost of Richmond Castle in a very dilapidated state, the unusually named 'Oliver Ducket' bastion. Sir Conyers D'Arcy had it rebuilt in castellated form as an eyecatcher.

CASTLE HOWARD. Temple of the Four Winds and Sham Fortifications (see below).

Left: *The Temple of the Four Winds, Castle Howard, North Yorkshire. Sir John Vanbrugh designed Castle Howard at the beginning of the eighteenth century and, with the help of Nicholas Hawksmoor, built the house and the buildings on the estate. At the time, it prompted Horace Walpole to write: 'I have seen gigantic places before, but never a sublime one.' Hawksmoor designed the superb mausoleum in the park but the Temple of the Winds was Vanbrugh's last building and was not completed until after his death in 1726. It has four Ionic porticoes, is topped by a dome and has a roofline embellished with urns and finials.*

Right: *The Sham Fortifications, Castle Howard, North Yorkshire. When approaching Castle Howard from the south or from the direction of Malton, the first intimation that you have reached the estate is when the road goes through Carrmire Gate, a low and rather narrow pedimented archway. There is no gate as such, and the archway is part of what is still the biggest folly in England, Vanbrugh's sham fortifications. These set the pattern for adding mock castle fronts to farms and other buildings for many years afterwards. The heavy, castellated wall has eleven fortified towers, some round, some square and some hexagonal, all crenellated and with machicolations – holes in the parapet for pouring boiling oil on possible attackers!*

Duncombe Park and Rievaulx Terraces, Helmsley, North Yorkshire. The gardens at Duncombe were started c.1713 and the long curving terrace, with the closed circular Doric Temple at one end and the open Ionic Rotunda (attributed to Vanbrugh) at the other, gives superb views of the surrounding countryside. The ruined Rievaulx Abbey, 3 miles up the valley, was also owned by the Duncombe family and in 1758 Thomas Duncombe II built what is known as the Rievaulx Terrace – again with temples at each end – and from it there are vistas of the abbey along specially cut paths through the trees. The National Trust now administers the terrace and the Ionic Temple (illustrated here) is furnished and decorated as a dining-room. It was used by the family for picnics; the guide book mentions that visitors are welcome to picnic but, of course, only on the terrace!

GREWELTHORPE. Hackfall Woods, a few miles north-west of Ripon, are full of neglected follies: there is Fisher's Hall (a pavilion), Mowbray Castle (a sham ruin) and Mowbray Point Banqueting House. These, together with one or two minor follies, were created by William Aislabie in the 1750s and Hackfall became one of the first great show gardens in England. All the follies are in a very dilapidated state and a trust has been set up to try to preserve them.

GRIMSTON PARK. Here there is a square tower on Wharfe Bank which was built c.1860. It stands 41 feet (13 metres) high and has an eight-sided lantern on an overhanging platform.

HARROGATE. Harlow Tower was erected in 1829 and in the 1950s the Harrogate Corporation converted it into an observation tower in a public park.

HELMSLEY. There are temples in Duncombe Park and on the Rievaulx Terrace (see above).

ILTON, near Masham. The Druid's Temple (see page 11).

PATELEY BRIDGE. Yorke's Folly, or 'Two Stoops' as it is known locally, was built by John Yorke on Guy's Cliff overlooking the town. Of the three pillars put up c.1800 to provide employment, only two remain; in 1893 a fierce gale blew the other one down.

The Octagon Tower, Fountains Abbey and Studley Royal Water Garden, near Ripon, North Yorkshire. The magnificent water gardens at Studley Royal were laid out by John Aislabie and his son William from about 1721, when they made use of the twisting valley of the River Skell to compose a linked series of gardens with picturesque views culminating in a view of the genuine ruins of Fountains Abbey. In 1983 the National Trust, which already owned the abbey, acquired the Studley Royal gardens with its Temple of Piety overlooking the so-called Moon Ponds, the Fishing Pavilions on either side of the river, Anne Boleyn's Seat, a grotto, the Temple of Fame, the Banqueting House and the Octagon Tower. The tower was originally a classical pavilion and it was William Aislabie who, in 1738, transformed it into a Gothic belvedere on top of a mound.

STUDLEY ROYAL. The Octagon Tower, Fountains Abbey and the Water Garden (see opposite).

TUPGILL PARK, Coverdale. 'The Forbidden Corner' garden is a modern theme park devised by Malcolm Tempest in Colin Armstrong's garden. After a public inquiry, in 2000 it was opened to the public and Forbidden Corner describes itself as a 'unique labyrinth of tunnels, chambers, follies and surprises'.

YORKSHIRE, SOUTH

BURGHWALLIS. Robin Hood's Well stands at the side of the A1 between Doncaster and Pontefract. Its square superstructure of huge stones has arches on three sides and it is attributed to Sir John Vanbrugh.

HOYLAND. Hoyland Lowe Stand is an eighteenth-century two-storey square tower which can be reached from the B6096 by a footpath.

PENISTONE. Hartcliff Tower is a ruined circular stone tower, 2 miles south-west of the town, on the edge of the Don valley. It is said to have been built c.1851.

WENTWORTH CASTLE. What was originally named 'Stainborough Castle', standing in the Wentworth Castle estate, is now called 'Wentworth Castle' and was seen in the BBC's *Restoration* programme in 2003. It is not accessible to the public. Steeple Lodge – in the form of a church tower - is the only folly that can be seen from the road, because it stands at the main entrance.

WENTWORTH WOODHOUSE. Although it is said that the two Wentworths cannot be considered separately, there are a number of follies on this estate which are now in the care of the Fitzwilliam Wentworth Amenity Trust. They include Keppel's Column and Hoober Stand (see below) and the Needle's Eye (see page 63).

Left: *Keppel's Column, Wentworth Woodhouse, South Yorkshire. Admiral Keppel was a friend of the Marquis of Rockingham, who considered that the admiral had been unfairly court-martialled following his naval defeat by the French at the Battle of Ushant in 1778. Keppel was acquitted and the Marquis decided to build this column in his honour in 1779. It is 136 feet (41 metres) high but it was intended that it should be taller and surmounted by Keppel's statue.*

Right: *Hoober Stand, Wentworth Woodhouse, South Yorkshire. Constructed in 1748, this unusually tapered tower was built to celebrate the victory at the Battle of Culloden against the Jacobite army of Prince Charles Edward Stuart. The tower is 518 feet (158 metres) above sea level and from the viewing platform on the top there is a magnificent view.*

The Gothic Temple, Bramham Park, near Wetherby, West Yorkshire. Begun in 1699, the grounds at Bramham Park were laid out in the French style by Robert Benson, first Lord Bingley, and are reminiscent of Versailles and Vaux-le-Vicomte, designed by Le Nôtre. The buildings were added later, between 1750 and 1770, for George Fox Lane (Lord Bingley's son-in-law) and the majority of these are attributed to James Paine. The Gothic Temple or Octagon was built in 1750 and stands on an open stretch of greensward known as the Bowling Green. Used as a summerhouse and a water tower at different periods of its history, it was more or less surrounded by trees until the disastrous storm of February 1962 when four hundred of them were destroyed.

YORKSHIRE, WEST

BINGLEY. St David's Ruin is a sham castle and an eyecatcher for St Ives House, across the Harden Valley, near Bingley. It was built by Benjamin Ferrand in 1796.

BRAMHAM PARK, near Wetherby. The Gothic Temple (see above).

HALIFAX. Wainhouse Tower is a prominent landmark overlooking Halifax and now belongs to the Borough of Calderdale. In 1871, John Wainhouse planned a tall

chimney for his Washer Lane dyeworks to reduce smoke pollution. Before the tower was finished, however, he sold the dyeworks and, as the new owner did not want the chimney, the building was completed as an observatory. The chimney is surrounded by a circular staircase inside the outer stone casing.

HUDDERSFIELD. The Jubilee Tower (see left).

The Jubilee Tower, Huddersfield, West Yorkshire. The Jubilee Tower was built on a hill on the outskirts of Huddersfield to celebrate Queen Victoria's Diamond Jubilee in 1897 and consequently it is also known as the Victoria Tower. It is a popular tourist attraction, with a fine view from the top.

Scotland

ALVES, Moray. York Tower is said to mark the site of the 'blasted heath', the meeting-place of Macbeth with the three 'secret, black and midnight hags'. Be that as it may, the embattled tower was built by Alexander Forteath in 1827 to commemorate the Duke of York.

BLAIR ATHOLL, Perth & Kinross. The Whim is a sham fort eyecatcher, only one wall thick, which was built for the second Duke of Atholl at Blair Castle in 1762.

BRIDGEND, Perth & Kinross. The Tower on Kinnoull Hill was built by the ninth Earl of Kinnoull after a tour of the Continent early in the nineteenth century. It is said that when he returned he wanted to simulate the grandeur of the Rhine castles with one overlooking the River Tay.

COLINSBURGH, Fife. After twenty-one years in India, the Honourable Robert Lindsay returned to Scotland in 1789 to farm for the next thirty-five years. In his old age he employed James Fisher in 1813 to build him an eyecatcher on Balcarres Crag. This embattled tower can easily be seen from the road out of Colinsburgh to Pittenweem.

DUNMORE, Falkirk. The Pineapple (see front cover; description on page 2).

EDINBURGH. Calton Hill overlooks the city and on it is a collection of buildings and statuary commemorating a number of great men. There is the pentangular monument to Lord Nelson, completed in 1816, but the most spectacular is what is known as 'The National Monument' although it was never completed because after 1829 funds ran out. It is known locally as 'the Disgrace of Edinburgh'.

EDZELL, Angus. The Dalhousie Arch (see below).

ELIE, Fife. The Lady's Tower is a bath-house built in the middle of the eighteenth century so that Lady Jane Anstruther of Elie House could change and bathe unobserved in a specially cut-away chamber below. 'Peeping Toms' were warned off by a servant with a bell!

The Dalhousie Arch, Edzell, Angus, straddles the main road into Edzell, erected by the local tenantry in 1887 in honour of the thirteenth Earl Dalhousie.

McCaig's Folly, Oban, Argyll. John Stuart McCaig, a rich Oban banker, had the laudable and practical Victorian aim of employing and subsequently educating the local unemployed. Between 1897 and 1900 he built what is known as McCaig's Folly – supposedly resembling the Colosseum in Rome, which he had seen on a tour of Italy. Not only did his memory fail him as to the design – his arches are Gothic, not classical – but his original plans for a museum and art gallery inside the building came to nothing.

FORRES, Moray. The Nelson Monument is believed to be the earliest monument to celebrate Nelson's victory at Trafalgar in 1805. This 1806 embattled tower – housing a Nelson museum – was designed by Charles Stuart, who was a local architect.

HADDINGTON, East Lothian. The Hopetoun Monument (see page 12).

MELLERSTAIN, Scottish Borders. The Hundy Mundy is an eyecatcher for Mellerstain House, near Kelso, and stands amid an avenue of trees about 2 miles south of the house. The folly was built by Robert Adam for George Baillie in 1778 and is accessible through the trees only when the cornfield surrounding it has been harvested.

OBAN, Argyll & Bute. McCaig's Folly (see above).

THURSO, Highland. Castle Lodge (see below).

The Castle Lodge, Thurso Castle, Highland. The lodge to Thurso Castle is a square, embattled block with a tower on one corner and turrets on the others, all with exaggerated crenellations, echoed by those on the adjacent gate. The complex is attributed to Donald Leed, who was the estate architect between 1870 and 1880.

Wales

DEVIL'S BRIDGE, Ceredigion. George III had reigned for fifty years in 1810 and Thomas Johnes erected an arch – the only one surviving of three – on his Hafod estate to celebrate the King's Golden Jubilee.

GLYNLLIFON, Gwynedd. Fort Williamsbourg (see below).

Fort Williamsbourg, Glynllifon, Gwynedd, stands in the park of Glynllifon College and was originally built in the late eighteenth century by Sir Thomas Wynn. He enlarged it into a real fort during the threat of a French invasion but it was never put to the test. It has been restored and has a plaque reading 'Williamsbourg Fort' over the door.

LLANARTHNEY, Carmarthenshire. Paxton's Tower, now in the guardianship of the National Trust, was built by Sir William Paxton in 1805 and there are inscriptions in Latin, Welsh and English stating that the building was erected as a tribute to Nelson, commemorating his victories and death in the service of his country.

LLANFROTHEN, Gwynedd. Watch Tower at Plas Brondanw (see right).

LLANGATTOCK, Monmouthshire. Clytha Castle stands on the north face of a low hill overlooking the road to Abergavenny from Monmouth (see page 62).

MOEL FAMAU, Denbighshire. The Jubilee Tower, standing nearly 2000 feet above sea

The Watch Tower at Plas Brondanw, Llanfrothen, Gwynedd. Sir Clough Williams-Ellis, the creator of Portmeirion, relates in his autobiography how this tower came into being – it was a wedding present from his fellow officers in the Welsh Guards after he asked for a 'ruin'! Headley adds that there is a plaque on it with the history of the folly together with the comment 'In the Second World War it was prepared as a local military strongpoint to repel the expected German invasion'.

Clytha Castle, Llangattock, Monmouthshire, was erected in 1790 by William Jones after the death of his wife and was designed by a little-known architect, John Davenport, with perhaps some help from his client. The castle is now in the hands of the Landmark Trust as a holiday home, and on one wall there is a tablet telling the sad story of why it was built, reading in part: 'Erected in the year 1790 by William Jones of Clytha House, husband of Elizabeth, last surviving child of Sir William Morgan of Tredegar, it was undertaken for the purpose of relieving a mind sincerely afflicted by the loss of a most excellent wife, to the memory of whose virtues this tablet is dedicated.'

level, was built to commemorate the Golden Jubilee of King George III in 1810. Although 'well advanced' in 1812, it was never quite finished. In 1862 it was blown down in a terrific storm. The stump of it remains, open to visitors.

MOLD, Flintshire. The embattled Sham Castle was built by Benjamin Gummow around 1800 as an eyecatcher for Nercwys Hall, which is a few miles south of Mold.

MONMOUTH, Monmouthshire. The Round House, built in 1794 on a hill called Kymin, was the favourite resort of a local dining club which, after much discussion, decided to build a Naval Monument nearby. This was erected in 1800, bearing plaques commemorating a number of admirals who had distinguished themselves in recent wars. Lord Nelson was once a guest of the club.

NEATH, Neath Port Talbot. Ivy Tower, built at the very end of the eighteenth century (builder unknown), is a circular castellated belvedere overlooking Neath. Although now just a shell, at one time it was used for banquets.

OLD COLWYN, Conwy. The nineteenth-century Woodall's Folly is a miniature sham castle in Tan-y-Coed Gardens. The local council, being unable to afford its repair, sold it to the Clwyd Historical Buildings Preservation Trust for just £1 in 1993. The Trust restored it as a house.

PONTYPRIDD, Rhondda Cynon Taff. The Glyntaff Druid Towers are all that was completed of a Druidic temple planned by Dr William Price in 1838. They are now part of a row of cottages.